This notebook belongs to:

_____

Published by: Character Designs

COMPETITIVE ANALYSIS

DATE: _____   COMPETITOR A: _____

UX PROJECT NAME: _____   COMPETITOR B: _____

FACTOR	MY BUSINESS	STRENGTH	WEAKNESS	COMPETITOR A	COMPETITOR B
Products					
Price					
Quality					
Selection					
Service					
Reliability					
Stability					
Expertise					
Company Reputation					
Location					
Appearance					
Sales Method					
Credit Policies					
Advertising					
Image					

COMPETITIVE ANALYSIS

DATE : _____   COMPETITOR A: _____

UX PROJECT NAME: _____   COMPETITOR B : _____

FACTOR	MY BUSINESS	STRENGTH	WEAKNESS	COMPETITOR A	COMPETITOR B
Products					
Price					
Quality					
Selection					
Service					
Reliability					
Stability					
Expertise					
Company Reputation					
Location					
Appearance					
Sales Method					
Credit Policies					
Advertising					
Image					

COMPETITIVE ANALYSIS

DATE: _____   COMPETITOR A: _____

UX PROJECT NAME: _____   COMPETITOR B: _____

FACTOR	MY BUSINESS	STRENGTH	WEAKNESS	COMPETITOR A	COMPETITOR B
Products					
Price					
Quality					
Selection					
Service					
Reliability					
Stability					
Expertise					
Company Reputation					
Location					
Appearance					
Sales Method					
Credit Policies					
Advertising					
Image					

COMPETITIVE ANALYSIS

DATE: _____

COMPETITOR A: _____

UX PROJECT NAME: _____

COMPETITOR B: _____

FACTOR	MY BUSINESS	STRENGTH	WEAKNESS	COMPETITOR A	COMPETITOR B
Products					
Price					
Quality					
Selection					
Service					
Reliability					
Stability					
Expertise					
Company Reputation					
Location					
Appearance					
Sales Method					
Credit Policies					
Advertising					
Image					

COMPETITIVE ANALYSIS

DATE: _____   COMPETITOR A: _____

UX PROJECT NAME: _____   COMPETITOR B: _____

FACTOR	MY BUSINESS	STRENGTH	WEAKNESS	COMPETITOR A	COMPETITOR B
Products					
Price					
Quality					
Selection					
Service					
Reliability					
Stability					
Expertise					
Company Reputation					
Location					
Appearance					
Sales Method					
Credit Policies					
Advertising					
Image					

COMPETITIVE ANALYSIS

DATE : _____

UX PROJECT NAME: _____

COMPETITOR A: _____

COMPETITOR B : _____

FACTOR	MY BUSINESS	STRENGTH	WEAKNESS	COMPETITOR A	COMPETITOR B
Products					
Price					
Quality					
Selection					
Service					
Reliability					
Stability					
Expertise					
Company Reputation					
Location					
Appearance					
Sales Method					
Credit Policies					
Advertising					
Image					

COMPETITIVE ANALYSIS

DATE: _____

COMPETITOR A: _____

UX PROJECT NAME: _____

COMPETITOR B: _____

FACTOR	MY BUSINESS	STRENGTH	WEAKNESS	COMPETITOR A	COMPETITOR B
Products					
Price					
Quality					
Selection					
Service					
Reliability					
Stability					
Expertise					
Company Reputation					
Location					
Appearance					
Sales Method					
Credit Policies					
Advertising					
Image					

COMPETITIVE ANALYSIS

DATE: _____

COMPETITOR A: _____

UX PROJECT NAME: _____

COMPETITOR B: _____

FACTOR	MY BUSINESS	STRENGTH	WEAKNESS	COMPETITOR A	COMPETITOR B
Products					
Price					
Quality					
Selection					
Service					
Reliability					
Stability					
Expertise					
Company Reputation					
Location					
Appearance					
Sales Method					
Credit Policies					
Advertising					
Image					

COMPETITIVE ANALYSIS

DATE: _____   COMPETITOR A: _____

UX PROJECT NAME: _____   COMPETITOR B: _____

FACTOR	MY BUSINESS	STRENGTH	WEAKNESS	COMPETITOR A	COMPETITOR B
Products					
Price					
Quality					
Selection					
Service					
Reliability					
Stability					
Expertise					
Company Reputation					
Location					
Appearance					
Sales Method					
Credit Policies					
Advertising					
Image					

COMPETITIVE ANALYSIS

DATE: _____

UX PROJECT NAME: _____

COMPETITOR A: _____

COMPETITOR B: _____

FACTOR	MY BUSINESS	STRENGTH	WEAKNESS	COMPETITOR A	COMPETITOR B
Products					
Price					
Quality					
Selection					
Service					
Reliability					
Stability					
Expertise					
Company Reputation					
Location					
Appearance					
Sales Method					
Credit Policies					
Advertising					
Image					

COMPETITIVE ANALYSIS

DATE: _____

COMPETITOR A: _____

UX PROJECT NAME: _____

COMPETITOR B: _____

FACTOR	MY BUSINESS	STRENGTH	WEAKNESS	COMPETITOR A	COMPETITOR B
Products					
Price					
Quality					
Selection					
Service					
Reliability					
Stability					
Expertise					
Company Reputation					
Location					
Appearance					
Sales Method					
Credit Policies					
Advertising					
Image					

COMPETITIVE ANALYSIS

DATE: _____

UX PROJECT NAME: _____

COMPETITOR A: _____

COMPETITOR B: _____

FACTOR	MY BUSINESS	STRENGTH	WEAKNESS	COMPETITOR A	COMPETITOR B
Products					
Price					
Quality					
Selection					
Service					
Reliability					
Stability					
Expertise					
Company Reputation					
Location					
Appearance					
Sales Method					
Credit Policies					
Advertising					
Image					

COMPETITIVE ANALYSIS

DATE: _____

COMPETITOR A: _____

UX PROJECT NAME: _____

COMPETITOR B: _____

FACTOR	MY BUSINESS	STRENGTH	WEAKNESS	COMPETITOR A	COMPETITOR B
Products					
Price					
Quality					
Selection					
Service					
Reliability					
Stability					
Expertise					
Company Reputation					
Location					
Appearance					
Sales Method					
Credit Policies					
Advertising					
Image					

COMPETITIVE ANALYSIS

DATE: _____

UX PROJECT NAME: _____

COMPETITOR A: _____

COMPETITOR B: _____

FACTOR	MY BUSINESS	STRENGTH	WEAKNESS	COMPETITOR A	COMPETITOR B
Products					
Price					
Quality					
Selection					
Service					
Reliability					
Stability					
Expertise					
Company Reputation					
Location					
Appearance					
Sales Method					
Credit Policies					
Advertising					
Image					

COMPETITIVE ANALYSIS

DATE : _____   COMPETITOR A : _____

UX PROJECT NAME: _____   COMPETITOR B : _____

FACTOR	MY BUSINESS	STRENGTH	WEAKNESS	COMPETITOR A	COMPETITOR B
Products					
Price					
Quality					
Selection					
Service					
Reliability					
Stability					
Expertise					
Company Reputation					
Location					
Appearance					
Sales Method					
Credit Policies					
Advertising					
Image					

COMPETITIVE ANALYSIS

DATE: _____

UX PROJECT NAME: _____

COMPETITOR A: _____

COMPETITOR B: _____

FACTOR	MY BUSINESS	STRENGTH	WEAKNESS	COMPETITOR A	COMPETITOR B
Products					
Price					
Quality					
Selection					
Service					
Reliability					
Stability					
Expertise					
Company Reputation					
Location					
Appearance					
Sales Method					
Credit Policies					
Advertising					
Image					

COMPETITIVE ANALYSIS

DATE: _____

COMPETITOR A: _____

UX PROJECT NAME: _____

COMPETITOR B: _____

FACTOR	MY BUSINESS	STRENGTH	WEAKNESS	COMPETITOR A	COMPETITOR B
Products					
Price					
Quality					
Selection					
Service					
Reliability					
Stability					
Expertise					
Company Reputation					
Location					
Appearance					
Sales Method					
Credit Policies					
Advertising					
Image					

COMPETITIVE ANALYSIS

DATE: _____

UX PROJECT NAME: _____

COMPETITOR A: _____

COMPETITOR B: _____

FACTOR	MY BUSINESS	STRENGTH	WEAKNESS	COMPETITOR A	COMPETITOR B
Products					
Price					
Quality					
Selection					
Service					
Reliability					
Stability					
Expertise					
Company Reputation					
Location					
Appearance					
Sales Method					
Credit Policies					
Advertising					
Image					

COMPETITIVE ANALYSIS

DATE: _____

COMPETITOR A: _____

UX PROJECT NAME: _____

COMPETITOR B: _____

FACTOR	MY BUSINESS	STRENGTH	WEAKNESS	COMPETITOR A	COMPETITOR B
Products					
Price					
Quality					
Selection					
Service					
Reliability					
Stability					
Expertise					
Company Reputation					
Location					
Appearance					
Sales Method					
Credit Policies					
Advertising					
Image					

COMPETITIVE ANALYSIS

DATE: _____

COMPETITOR A: _____

UX PROJECT NAME: _____

COMPETITOR B: _____

FACTOR	MY BUSINESS	STRENGTH	WEAKNESS	COMPETITOR A	COMPETITOR B
Products					
Price					
Quality					
Selection					
Service					
Reliability					
Stability					
Expertise					
Company Reputation					
Location					
Appearance					
Sales Method					
Credit Policies					
Advertising					
Image					

COMPETITIVE ANALYSIS

DATE: _____   COMPETITOR A: _____

UX PROJECT NAME: _____   COMPETITOR B: _____

FACTOR	MY BUSINESS	STRENGTH	WEAKNESS	COMPETITOR A	COMPETITOR B
Products					
Price					
Quality					
Selection					
Service					
Reliability					
Stability					
Expertise					
Company Reputation					
Location					
Appearance					
Sales Method					
Credit Policies					
Advertising					
Image					

COMPETITIVE ANALYSIS

DATE: _____

COMPETITOR A: _____

UX PROJECT NAME: _____

COMPETITOR B: _____

FACTOR	MY BUSINESS	STRENGTH	WEAKNESS	COMPETITOR A	COMPETITOR B
Products					
Price					
Quality					
Selection					
Service					
Reliability					
Stability					
Expertise					
Company Reputation					
Location					
Appearance					
Sales Method					
Credit Policies					
Advertising					
Image					

COMPETITIVE ANALYSIS

DATE: _____

COMPETITOR A: _____

UX PROJECT NAME: _____

COMPETITOR B: _____

FACTOR	MY BUSINESS	STRENGTH	WEAKNESS	COMPETITOR A	COMPETITOR B
Products					
Price					
Quality					
Selection					
Service					
Reliability					
Stability					
Expertise					
Company Reputation					
Location					
Appearance					
Sales Method					
Credit Policies					
Advertising					
Image					

COMPETITIVE ANALYSIS

DATE: _____

COMPETITOR A: _____

UX PROJECT NAME: _____

COMPETITOR B: _____

FACTOR	MY BUSINESS	STRENGTH	WEAKNESS	COMPETITOR A	COMPETITOR B
Products					
Price					
Quality					
Selection					
Service					
Reliability					
Stability					
Expertise					
Company Reputation					
Location					
Appearance					
Sales Method					
Credit Policies					
Advertising					
Image					

COMPETITIVE ANALYSIS

DATE: _____   COMPETITOR A: _____

UX PROJECT NAME: _____   COMPETITOR B: _____

FACTOR	MY BUSINESS	STRENGTH	WEAKNESS	COMPETITOR A	COMPETITOR B
Products					
Price					
Quality					
Selection					
Service					
Reliability					
Stability					
Expertise					
Company Reputation					
Location					
Appearance					
Sales Method					
Credit Policies					
Advertising					
Image					

COMPETITIVE ANALYSIS

DATE: _____

COMPETITOR A: _____

UX PROJECT NAME: _____

COMPETITOR B: _____

FACTOR	MY BUSINESS	STRENGTH	WEAKNESS	COMPETITOR A	COMPETITOR B
Products					
Price					
Quality					
Selection					
Service					
Reliability					
Stability					
Expertise					
Company Reputation					
Location					
Appearance					
Sales Method					
Credit Policies					
Advertising					
Image					

COMPETITIVE ANALYSIS

DATE: _____   COMPETITOR A: _____

UX PROJECT NAME: _____   COMPETITOR B: _____

FACTOR	MY BUSINESS	STRENGTH	WEAKNESS	COMPETITOR A	COMPETITOR B
Products					
Price					
Quality					
Selection					
Service					
Reliability					
Stability					
Expertise					
Company Reputation					
Location					
Appearance					
Sales Method					
Credit Policies					
Advertising					
Image					

COMPETITIVE ANALYSIS

DATE: _____

COMPETITOR A: _____

UX PROJECT NAME: _____

COMPETITOR B: _____

FACTOR	MY BUSINESS	STRENGTH	WEAKNESS	COMPETITOR A	COMPETITOR B
Products					
Price					
Quality					
Selection					
Service					
Reliability					
Stability					
Expertise					
Company Reputation					
Location					
Appearance					
Sales Method					
Credit Policies					
Advertising					
Image					

COMPETITIVE ANALYSIS

DATE: _____   COMPETITOR A: _____

UX PROJECT NAME: _____   COMPETITOR B: _____

FACTOR	MY BUSINESS	STRENGTH	WEAKNESS	COMPETITOR A	COMPETITOR B
Products					
Price					
Quality					
Selection					
Service					
Reliability					
Stability					
Expertise					
Company Reputation					
Location					
Appearance					
Sales Method					
Credit Policies					
Advertising					
Image					

COMPETITIVE ANALYSIS

DATE: _____

UX PROJECT NAME: _____

COMPETITOR A: _____

COMPETITOR B: _____

FACTOR	MY BUSINESS	STRENGTH	WEAKNESS	COMPETITOR A	COMPETITOR B
Products					
Price					
Quality					
Selection					
Service					
Reliability					
Stability					
Expertise					
Company Reputation					
Location					
Appearance					
Sales Method					
Credit Policies					
Advertising					
Image					

COMPETITIVE ANALYSIS

DATE: _____   COMPETITOR A: _____

UX PROJECT NAME: _____   COMPETITOR B: _____

FACTOR	MY BUSINESS	STRENGTH	WEAKNESS	COMPETITOR A	COMPETITOR B
Products					
Price					
Quality					
Selection					
Service					
Reliability					
Stability					
Expertise					
Company Reputation					
Location					
Appearance					
Sales Method					
Credit Policies					
Advertising					
Image					

COMPETITIVE ANALYSIS

DATE: _____

COMPETITOR A: _____

UX PROJECT NAME: _____

COMPETITOR B: _____

FACTOR	MY BUSINESS	STRENGTH	WEAKNESS	COMPETITOR A	COMPETITOR B
Products					
Price					
Quality					
Selection					
Service					
Reliability					
Stability					
Expertise					
Company Reputation					
Location					
Appearance					
Sales Method					
Credit Policies					
Advertising					
Image					

COMPETITIVE ANALYSIS

DATE: _____

COMPETITOR A: _____

UX PROJECT NAME: _____

COMPETITOR B: _____

FACTOR	MY BUSINESS	STRENGTH	WEAKNESS	COMPETITOR A	COMPETITOR B
Products					
Price					
Quality					
Selection					
Service					
Reliability					
Stability					
Expertise					
Company Reputation					
Location					
Appearance					
Sales Method					
Credit Policies					
Advertising					
Image					

COMPETITIVE ANALYSIS

DATE: _____

UX PROJECT NAME: _____

COMPETITOR A: _____

COMPETITOR B: _____

FACTOR	MY BUSINESS	STRENGTH	WEAKNESS	COMPETITOR A	COMPETITOR B
Products					
Price					
Quality					
Selection					
Service					
Reliability					
Stability					
Expertise					
Company Reputation					
Location					
Appearance					
Sales Method					
Credit Policies					
Advertising					
Image					

COMPETITIVE ANALYSIS

DATE : _____   COMPETITOR A : _____

UX PROJECT NAME: _____   COMPETITOR B : _____

FACTOR	MY BUSINESS	STRENGTH	WEAKNESS	COMPETITOR A	COMPETITOR B
Products					
Price					
Quality					
Selection					
Service					
Reliability					
Stability					
Expertise					
Company Reputation					
Location					
Appearance					
Sales Method					
Credit Policies					
Advertising					
Image					

COMPETITIVE ANALYSIS

DATE : _____   COMPETITOR A : _____

UX PROJECT NAME : _____   COMPETITOR B : _____

FACTOR	MY BUSINESS	STRENGTH	WEAKNESS	COMPETITOR A	COMPETITOR B
Products					
Price					
Quality					
Selection					
Service					
Reliability					
Stability					
Expertise					
Company Reputation					
Location					
Appearance					
Sales Method					
Credit Policies					
Advertising					
Image					

COMPETITIVE ANALYSIS

DATE: _____

COMPETITOR A: _____

UX PROJECT NAME: _____

COMPETITOR B: _____

FACTOR	MY BUSINESS	STRENGTH	WEAKNESS	COMPETITOR A	COMPETITOR B
Products					
Price					
Quality					
Selection					
Service					
Reliability					
Stability					
Expertise					
Company Reputation					
Location					
Appearance					
Sales Method					
Credit Policies					
Advertising					
Image					

COMPETITIVE ANALYSIS

DATE: _____   COMPETITOR A: _____

UX PROJECT NAME: _____   COMPETITOR B: _____

FACTOR	MY BUSINESS	STRENGTH	WEAKNESS	COMPETITOR A	COMPETITOR B
Products					
Price					
Quality					
Selection					
Service					
Reliability					
Stability					
Expertise					
Company Reputation					
Location					
Appearance					
Sales Method					
Credit Policies					
Advertising					
Image					

COMPETITIVE ANALYSIS

DATE: _____   COMPETITOR A: _____

UX PROJECT NAME: _____   COMPETITOR B: _____

FACTOR	MY BUSINESS	STRENGTH	WEAKNESS	COMPETITOR A	COMPETITOR B
Products					
Price					
Quality					
Selection					
Service					
Reliability					
Stability					
Expertise					
Company Reputation					
Location					
Appearance					
Sales Method					
Credit Policies					
Advertising					
Image					

COMPETITIVE ANALYSIS

DATE: _____   COMPETITOR A: _____

UX PROJECT NAME: _____   COMPETITOR B: _____

FACTOR	MY BUSINESS	STRENGTH	WEAKNESS	COMPETITOR A	COMPETITOR B
Products					
Price					
Quality					
Selection					
Service					
Reliability					
Stability					
Expertise					
Company Reputation					
Location					
Appearance					
Sales Method					
Credit Policies					
Advertising					
Image					

COMPETITIVE ANALYSIS

DATE: _____

UX PROJECT NAME: _____

COMPETITOR A: _____

COMPETITOR B: _____

FACTOR	MY BUSINESS	STRENGTH	WEAKNESS	COMPETITOR A	COMPETITOR B
Products					
Price					
Quality					
Selection					
Service					
Reliability					
Stability					
Expertise					
Company Reputation					
Location					
Appearance					
Sales Method					
Credit Policies					
Advertising					
Image					

COMPETITIVE ANALYSIS

DATE: _____

COMPETITOR A: _____

UX PROJECT NAME: _____

COMPETITOR B: _____

FACTOR	MY BUSINESS	STRENGTH	WEAKNESS	COMPETITOR A	COMPETITOR B
Products					
Price					
Quality					
Selection					
Service					
Reliability					
Stability					
Expertise					
Company Reputation					
Location					
Appearance					
Sales Method					
Credit Policies					
Advertising					
Image					

COMPETITIVE ANALYSIS

DATE: _____

COMPETITOR A: _____

UX PROJECT NAME: _____

COMPETITOR B: _____

FACTOR	MY BUSINESS	STRENGTH	WEAKNESS	COMPETITOR A	COMPETITOR B
Products					
Price					
Quality					
Selection					
Service					
Reliability					
Stability					
Expertise					
Company Reputation					
Location					
Appearance					
Sales Method					
Credit Policies					
Advertising					
Image					

COMPETITIVE ANALYSIS

DATE: _____

UX PROJECT NAME: _____

COMPETITOR A: _____

COMPETITOR B: _____

FACTOR	MY BUSINESS	STRENGTH	WEAKNESS	COMPETITOR A	COMPETITOR B
Products					
Price					
Quality					
Selection					
Service					
Reliability					
Stability					
Expertise					
Company Reputation					
Location					
Appearance					
Sales Method					
Credit Policies					
Advertising					
Image					

COMPETITIVE ANALYSIS

DATE: _____

COMPETITOR A: _____

UX PROJECT NAME: _____

COMPETITOR B: _____

FACTOR	MY BUSINESS	STRENGTH	WEAKNESS	COMPETITOR A	COMPETITOR B
Products					
Price					
Quality					
Selection					
Service					
Reliability					
Stability					
Expertise					
Company Reputation					
Location					
Appearance					
Sales Method					
Credit Policies					
Advertising					
Image					

COMPETITIVE ANALYSIS

DATE: _____

COMPETITOR A: _____

UX PROJECT NAME: _____

COMPETITOR B: _____

FACTOR	MY BUSINESS	STRENGTH	WEAKNESS	COMPETITOR A	COMPETITOR B
Products					
Price					
Quality					
Selection					
Service					
Reliability					
Stability					
Expertise					
Company Reputation					
Location					
Appearance					
Sales Method					
Credit Policies					
Advertising					
Image					

COMPETITIVE ANALYSIS

DATE : _____   COMPETITOR A : _____

UX PROJECT NAME: _____   COMPETITOR B : _____

FACTOR	MY BUSINESS	STRENGTH	WEAKNESS	COMPETITOR A	COMPETITOR B
Products					
Price					
Quality					
Selection					
Service					
Reliability					
Stability					
Expertise					
Company Reputation					
Location					
Appearance					
Sales Method					
Credit Policies					
Advertising					
Image					

COMPETITIVE ANALYSIS

DATE: _____

COMPETITOR A: _____

UX PROJECT NAME: _____

COMPETITOR B: _____

FACTOR	MY BUSINESS	STRENGTH	WEAKNESS	COMPETITOR A	COMPETITOR B
Products					
Price					
Quality					
Selection					
Service					
Reliability					
Stability					
Expertise					
Company Reputation					
Location					
Appearance					
Sales Method					
Credit Policies					
Advertising					
Image					

COMPETITIVE ANALYSIS

DATE : _____   COMPETITOR A : _____

UX PROJECT NAME: _____   COMPETITOR B : _____

FACTOR	MY BUSINESS	STRENGTH	WEAKNESS	COMPETITOR A	COMPETITOR B
Products					
Price					
Quality					
Selection					
Service					
Reliability					
Stability					
Expertise					
Company Reputation					
Location					
Appearance					
Sales Method					
Credit Policies					
Advertising					
Image					

COMPETITIVE ANALYSIS

DATE: _____

COMPETITOR A: _____

UX PROJECT NAME: _____

COMPETITOR B: _____

FACTOR	MY BUSINESS	STRENGTH	WEAKNESS	COMPETITOR A	COMPETITOR B
Products					
Price					
Quality					
Selection					
Service					
Reliability					
Stability					
Expertise					
Company Reputation					
Location					
Appearance					
Sales Method					
Credit Policies					
Advertising					
Image					

COMPETITIVE ANALYSIS

DATE : _____

COMPETITOR A : _____

UX PROJECT NAME: _____

COMPETITOR B : _____

FACTOR	MY BUSINESS	STRENGTH	WEAKNESS	COMPETITOR A	COMPETITOR B
Products					
Price					
Quality					
Selection					
Service					
Reliability					
Stability					
Expertise					
Company Reputation					
Location					
Appearance					
Sales Method					
Credit Policies					
Advertising					
Image					

COMPETITIVE ANALYSIS

DATE: _____

COMPETITOR A: _____

UX PROJECT NAME: _____

COMPETITOR B: _____

FACTOR	MY BUSINESS	STRENGTH	WEAKNESS	COMPETITOR A	COMPETITOR B
Products					
Price					
Quality					
Selection					
Service					
Reliability					
Stability					
Expertise					
Company Reputation					
Location					
Appearance					
Sales Method					
Credit Policies					
Advertising					
Image					

COMPETITIVE ANALYSIS

DATE: _____

COMPETITOR A: _____

UX PROJECT NAME: _____

COMPETITOR B: _____

FACTOR	MY BUSINESS	STRENGTH	WEAKNESS	COMPETITOR A	COMPETITOR B
Products					
Price					
Quality					
Selection					
Service					
Reliability					
Stability					
Expertise					
Company Reputation					
Location					
Appearance					
Sales Method					
Credit Policies					
Advertising					
Image					

COMPETITIVE ANALYSIS

DATE: _____

COMPETITOR A: _____

UX PROJECT NAME: _____

COMPETITOR B: _____

FACTOR	MY BUSINESS	STRENGTH	WEAKNESS	COMPETITOR A	COMPETITOR B
Products					
Price					
Quality					
Selection					
Service					
Reliability					
Stability					
Expertise					
Company Reputation					
Location					
Appearance					
Sales Method					
Credit Policies					
Advertising					
Image					

COMPETITIVE ANALYSIS

DATE: _____   COMPETITOR A: _____

UX PROJECT NAME: _____   COMPETITOR B: _____

FACTOR	MY BUSINESS	STRENGTH	WEAKNESS	COMPETITOR A	COMPETITOR B
Products					
Price					
Quality					
Selection					
Service					
Reliability					
Stability					
Expertise					
Company Reputation					
Location					
Appearance					
Sales Method					
Credit Policies					
Advertising					
Image					

COMPETITIVE ANALYSIS

DATE: _____

COMPETITOR A: _____

UX PROJECT NAME: _____

COMPETITOR B: _____

FACTOR	MY BUSINESS	STRENGTH	WEAKNESS	COMPETITOR A	COMPETITOR B
Products					
Price					
Quality					
Selection					
Service					
Reliability					
Stability					
Expertise					
Company Reputation					
Location					
Appearance					
Sales Method					
Credit Policies					
Advertising					
Image					

COMPETITIVE ANALYSIS

DATE: _____   COMPETITOR A: _____

UX PROJECT NAME: _____   COMPETITOR B: _____

FACTOR	MY BUSINESS	STRENGTH	WEAKNESS	COMPETITOR A	COMPETITOR B
Products					
Price					
Quality					
Selection					
Service					
Reliability					
Stability					
Expertise					
Company Reputation					
Location					
Appearance					
Sales Method					
Credit Policies					
Advertising					
Image					

COMPETITIVE ANALYSIS

DATE: _____   COMPETITOR A: _____

UX PROJECT NAME: _____   COMPETITOR B: _____

FACTOR	MY BUSINESS	STRENGTH	WEAKNESS	COMPETITOR A	COMPETITOR B
Products					
Price					
Quality					
Selection					
Service					
Reliability					
Stability					
Expertise					
Company Reputation					
Location					
Appearance					
Sales Method					
Credit Policies					
Advertising					
Image					

COMPETITIVE ANALYSIS

DATE: _____   COMPETITOR A: _____

UX PROJECT NAME: _____   COMPETITOR B: _____

FACTOR	MY BUSINESS	STRENGTH	WEAKNESS	COMPETITOR A	COMPETITOR B
Products					
Price					
Quality					
Selection					
Service					
Reliability					
Stability					
Expertise					
Company Reputation					
Location					
Appearance					
Sales Method					
Credit Policies					
Advertising					
Image					

COMPETITIVE ANALYSIS

DATE : _____   COMPETITOR A : _____

UX PROJECT NAME : _____   COMPETITOR B : _____

FACTOR	MY BUSINESS	STRENGTH	WEAKNESS	COMPETITOR A	COMPETITOR B
Products					
Price					
Quality					
Selection					
Service					
Reliability					
Stability					
Expertise					
Company Reputation					
Location					
Appearance					
Sales Method					
Credit Policies					
Advertising					
Image					

COMPETITIVE ANALYSIS

DATE: _____   COMPETITOR A: _____

UX PROJECT NAME: _____   COMPETITOR B: _____

FACTOR	MY BUSINESS	STRENGTH	WEAKNESS	COMPETITOR A	COMPETITOR B
Products					
Price					
Quality					
Selection					
Service					
Reliability					
Stability					
Expertise					
Company Reputation					
Location					
Appearance					
Sales Method					
Credit Policies					
Advertising					
Image					

COMPETITIVE ANALYSIS

DATE: _____

COMPETITOR A: _____

UX PROJECT NAME: _____

COMPETITOR B: _____

FACTOR	MY BUSINESS	STRENGTH	WEAKNESS	COMPETITOR A	COMPETITOR B
Products					
Price					
Quality					
Selection					
Service					
Reliability					
Stability					
Expertise					
Company Reputation					
Location					
Appearance					
Sales Method					
Credit Policies					
Advertising					
Image					

COMPETITIVE ANALYSIS

DATE: _____

COMPETITOR A: _____

UX PROJECT NAME: _____

COMPETITOR B: _____

FACTOR	MY BUSINESS	STRENGTH	WEAKNESS	COMPETITOR A	COMPETITOR B
Products					
Price					
Quality					
Selection					
Service					
Reliability					
Stability					
Expertise					
Company Reputation					
Location					
Appearance					
Sales Method					
Credit Policies					
Advertising					
Image					

COMPETITIVE ANALYSIS

DATE : _____

COMPETITOR A : _____

UX PROJECT NAME: _____

COMPETITOR B : _____

FACTOR	MY BUSINESS	STRENGTH	WEAKNESS	COMPETITOR A	COMPETITOR B
Products					
Price					
Quality					
Selection					
Service					
Reliability					
Stability					
Expertise					
Company Reputation					
Location					
Appearance					
Sales Method					
Credit Policies					
Advertising					
Image					

COMPETITIVE ANALYSIS

DATE: _____

COMPETITOR A: _____

UX PROJECT NAME: _____

COMPETITOR B: _____

FACTOR	MY BUSINESS	STRENGTH	WEAKNESS	COMPETITOR A	COMPETITOR B
Products					
Price					
Quality					
Selection					
Service					
Reliability					
Stability					
Expertise					
Company Reputation					
Location					
Appearance					
Sales Method					
Credit Policies					
Advertising					
Image					

COMPETITIVE ANALYSIS

DATE: _____

UX PROJECT NAME: _____

COMPETITOR A: _____

COMPETITOR B: _____

FACTOR	MY BUSINESS	STRENGTH	WEAKNESS	COMPETITOR A	COMPETITOR B
Products					
Price					
Quality					
Selection					
Service					
Reliability					
Stability					
Expertise					
Company Reputation					
Location					
Appearance					
Sales Method					
Credit Policies					
Advertising					
Image					

COMPETITIVE ANALYSIS

DATE: _____

COMPETITOR A: _____

UX PROJECT NAME: _____

COMPETITOR B: _____

FACTOR	MY BUSINESS	STRENGTH	WEAKNESS	COMPETITOR A	COMPETITOR B
Products					
Price					
Quality					
Selection					
Service					
Reliability					
Stability					
Expertise					
Company Reputation					
Location					
Appearance					
Sales Method					
Credit Policies					
Advertising					
Image					

COMPETITIVE ANALYSIS

DATE: _____

COMPETITOR A: _____

UX PROJECT NAME: _____

COMPETITOR B: _____

FACTOR	MY BUSINESS	STRENGTH	WEAKNESS	COMPETITOR A	COMPETITOR B
Products					
Price					
Quality					
Selection					
Service					
Reliability					
Stability					
Expertise					
Company Reputation					
Location					
Appearance					
Sales Method					
Credit Policies					
Advertising					
Image					

COMPETITIVE ANALYSIS

DATE: _____

COMPETITOR A: _____

UX PROJECT NAME: _____

COMPETITOR B: _____

FACTOR	MY BUSINESS	STRENGTH	WEAKNESS	COMPETITOR A	COMPETITOR B
Products					
Price					
Quality					
Selection					
Service					
Reliability					
Stability					
Expertise					
Company Reputation					
Location					
Appearance					
Sales Method					
Credit Policies					
Advertising					
Image					

COMPETITIVE ANALYSIS

DATE: _____   COMPETITOR A: _____

UX PROJECT NAME: _____   COMPETITOR B: _____

FACTOR	MY BUSINESS	STRENGTH	WEAKNESS	COMPETITOR A	COMPETITOR B
Products					
Price					
Quality					
Selection					
Service					
Reliability					
Stability					
Expertise					
Company Reputation					
Location					
Appearance					
Sales Method					
Credit Policies					
Advertising					
Image					

COMPETITIVE ANALYSIS

DATE: _____

COMPETITOR A: _____

UX PROJECT NAME: _____

COMPETITOR B: _____

FACTOR	MY BUSINESS	STRENGTH	WEAKNESS	COMPETITOR A	COMPETITOR B
Products					
Price					
Quality					
Selection					
Service					
Reliability					
Stability					
Expertise					
Company Reputation					
Location					
Appearance					
Sales Method					
Credit Policies					
Advertising					
Image					

COMPETITIVE ANALYSIS

DATE: _____

COMPETITOR A: _____

UX PROJECT NAME: _____

COMPETITOR B: _____

FACTOR	MY BUSINESS	STRENGTH	WEAKNESS	COMPETITOR A	COMPETITOR B
Products					
Price					
Quality					
Selection					
Service					
Reliability					
Stability					
Expertise					
Company Reputation					
Location					
Appearance					
Sales Method					
Credit Policies					
Advertising					
Image					

COMPETITIVE ANALYSIS

DATE: _____   COMPETITOR A: _____

UX PROJECT NAME: _____   COMPETITOR B: _____

FACTOR	MY BUSINESS	STRENGTH	WEAKNESS	COMPETITOR A	COMPETITOR B
Products					
Price					
Quality					
Selection					
Service					
Reliability					
Stability					
Expertise					
Company Reputation					
Location					
Appearance					
Sales Method					
Credit Policies					
Advertising					
Image					

COMPETITIVE ANALYSIS

DATE: _____

UX PROJECT NAME: _____

COMPETITOR A: _____

COMPETITOR B: _____

FACTOR	MY BUSINESS	STRENGTH	WEAKNESS	COMPETITOR A	COMPETITOR B
Products					
Price					
Quality					
Selection					
Service					
Reliability					
Stability					
Expertise					
Company Reputation					
Location					
Appearance					
Sales Method					
Credit Policies					
Advertising					
Image					

COMPETITIVE ANALYSIS

DATE: _____   COMPETITOR A: _____

UX PROJECT NAME: _____   COMPETITOR B: _____

FACTOR	MY BUSINESS	STRENGTH	WEAKNESS	COMPETITOR A	COMPETITOR B
Products					
Price					
Quality					
Selection					
Service					
Reliability					
Stability					
Expertise					
Company Reputation					
Location					
Appearance					
Sales Method					
Credit Policies					
Advertising					
Image					

COMPETITIVE ANALYSIS

DATE: _____

UX PROJECT NAME: _____

COMPETITOR A: _____

COMPETITOR B: _____

FACTOR	MY BUSINESS	STRENGTH	WEAKNESS	COMPETITOR A	COMPETITOR B
Products					
Price					
Quality					
Selection					
Service					
Reliability					
Stability					
Expertise					
Company Reputation					
Location					
Appearance					
Sales Method					
Credit Policies					
Advertising					
Image					

COMPETITIVE ANALYSIS

DATE: _____

COMPETITOR A: _____

UX PROJECT NAME: _____

COMPETITOR B: _____

FACTOR	MY BUSINESS	STRENGTH	WEAKNESS	COMPETITOR A	COMPETITOR B
Products					
Price					
Quality					
Selection					
Service					
Reliability					
Stability					
Expertise					
Company Reputation					
Location					
Appearance					
Sales Method					
Credit Policies					
Advertising					
Image					

COMPETITIVE ANALYSIS

DATE: _____   COMPETITOR A: _____

UX PROJECT NAME: _____   COMPETITOR B: _____

FACTOR	MY BUSINESS	STRENGTH	WEAKNESS	COMPETITOR A	COMPETITOR B
Products					
Price					
Quality					
Selection					
Service					
Reliability					
Stability					
Expertise					
Company Reputation					
Location					
Appearance					
Sales Method					
Credit Policies					
Advertising					
Image					

COMPETITIVE ANALYSIS

DATE : _____   COMPETITOR A : _____

UX PROJECT NAME : _____   COMPETITOR B : _____

FACTOR	MY BUSINESS	STRENGTH	WEAKNESS	COMPETITOR A	COMPETITOR B
Products					
Price					
Quality					
Selection					
Service					
Reliability					
Stability					
Expertise					
Company Reputation					
Location					
Appearance					
Sales Method					
Credit Policies					
Advertising					
Image					

COMPETITIVE ANALYSIS

DATE: _____

UX PROJECT NAME: _____

COMPETITOR A: _____

COMPETITOR B: _____

FACTOR	MY BUSINESS	STRENGTH	WEAKNESS	COMPETITOR A	COMPETITOR B
Products					
Price					
Quality					
Selection					
Service					
Reliability					
Stability					
Expertise					
Company Reputation					
Location					
Appearance					
Sales Method					
Credit Policies					
Advertising					
Image					

COMPETITIVE ANALYSIS

DATE: _____

COMPETITOR A: _____

UX PROJECT NAME: _____

COMPETITOR B: _____

FACTOR	MY BUSINESS	STRENGTH	WEAKNESS	COMPETITOR A	COMPETITOR B
Products					
Price					
Quality					
Selection					
Service					
Reliability					
Stability					
Expertise					
Company Reputation					
Location					
Appearance					
Sales Method					
Credit Policies					
Advertising					
Image					

COMPETITIVE ANALYSIS

DATE: _____

COMPETITOR A: _____

UX PROJECT NAME: _____

COMPETITOR B: _____

FACTOR	MY BUSINESS	STRENGTH	WEAKNESS	COMPETITOR A	COMPETITOR B
Products					
Price					
Quality					
Selection					
Service					
Reliability					
Stability					
Expertise					
Company Reputation					
Location					
Appearance					
Sales Method					
Credit Policies					
Advertising					
Image					

COMPETITIVE ANALYSIS

DATE: _____

UX PROJECT NAME: _____

COMPETITOR A: _____

COMPETITOR B: _____

FACTOR	MY BUSINESS	STRENGTH	WEAKNESS	COMPETITOR A	COMPETITOR B
Products					
Price					
Quality					
Selection					
Service					
Reliability					
Stability					
Expertise					
Company Reputation					
Location					
Appearance					
Sales Method					
Credit Policies					
Advertising					
Image					

COMPETITIVE ANALYSIS

DATE: _____

COMPETITOR A: _____

UX PROJECT NAME: _____

COMPETITOR B: _____

FACTOR	MY BUSINESS	STRENGTH	WEAKNESS	COMPETITOR A	COMPETITOR B
Products					
Price					
Quality					
Selection					
Service					
Reliability					
Stability					
Expertise					
Company Reputation					
Location					
Appearance					
Sales Method					
Credit Policies					
Advertising					
Image					

COMPETITIVE ANALYSIS

DATE: _____

COMPETITOR A: _____

UX PROJECT NAME: _____

COMPETITOR B: _____

FACTOR	MY BUSINESS	STRENGTH	WEAKNESS	COMPETITOR A	COMPETITOR B
Products					
Price					
Quality					
Selection					
Service					
Reliability					
Stability					
Expertise					
Company Reputation					
Location					
Appearance					
Sales Method					
Credit Policies					
Advertising					
Image					

COMPETITIVE ANALYSIS

DATE: _____   COMPETITOR A: _____

UX PROJECT NAME: _____   COMPETITOR B: _____

FACTOR	MY BUSINESS	STRENGTH	WEAKNESS	COMPETITOR A	COMPETITOR B
Products					
Price					
Quality					
Selection					
Service					
Reliability					
Stability					
Expertise					
Company Reputation					
Location					
Appearance					
Sales Method					
Credit Policies					
Advertising					
Image					

COMPETITIVE ANALYSIS

DATE: _____

COMPETITOR A: _____

UX PROJECT NAME: _____

COMPETITOR B: _____

FACTOR	MY BUSINESS	STRENGTH	WEAKNESS	COMPETITOR A	COMPETITOR B
Products					
Price					
Quality					
Selection					
Service					
Reliability					
Stability					
Expertise					
Company Reputation					
Location					
Appearance					
Sales Method					
Credit Policies					
Advertising					
Image					

COMPETITIVE ANALYSIS

DATE: _____

COMPETITOR A: _____

UX PROJECT NAME: _____

COMPETITOR B: _____

FACTOR	MY BUSINESS	STRENGTH	WEAKNESS	COMPETITOR A	COMPETITOR B
Products					
Price					
Quality					
Selection					
Service					
Reliability					
Stability					
Expertise					
Company Reputation					
Location					
Appearance					
Sales Method					
Credit Policies					
Advertising					
Image					

COMPETITIVE ANALYSIS

DATE: _____

COMPETITOR A: _____

UX PROJECT NAME: _____

COMPETITOR B: _____

FACTOR	MY BUSINESS	STRENGTH	WEAKNESS	COMPETITOR A	COMPETITOR B
Products					
Price					
Quality					
Selection					
Service					
Reliability					
Stability					
Expertise					
Company Reputation					
Location					
Appearance					
Sales Method					
Credit Policies					
Advertising					
Image					

COMPETITIVE ANALYSIS

DATE: _____

UX PROJECT NAME: _____

COMPETITOR A: _____

COMPETITOR B: _____

FACTOR	MY BUSINESS	STRENGTH	WEAKNESS	COMPETITOR A	COMPETITOR B
Products					
Price					
Quality					
Selection					
Service					
Reliability					
Stability					
Expertise					
Company Reputation					
Location					
Appearance					
Sales Method					
Credit Policies					
Advertising					
Image					

COMPETITIVE ANALYSIS

DATE: _____

COMPETITOR A: _____

UX PROJECT NAME: _____

COMPETITOR B: _____

FACTOR	MY BUSINESS	STRENGTH	WEAKNESS	COMPETITOR A	COMPETITOR B
Products					
Price					
Quality					
Selection					
Service					
Reliability					
Stability					
Expertise					
Company Reputation					
Location					
Appearance					
Sales Method					
Credit Policies					
Advertising					
Image					

COMPETITIVE ANALYSIS

DATE: _____

COMPETITOR A: _____

UX PROJECT NAME: _____

COMPETITOR B: _____

FACTOR	MY BUSINESS	STRENGTH	WEAKNESS	COMPETITOR A	COMPETITOR B
Products					
Price					
Quality					
Selection					
Service					
Reliability					
Stability					
Expertise					
Company Reputation					
Location					
Appearance					
Sales Method					
Credit Policies					
Advertising					
Image					

COMPETITIVE ANALYSIS

DATE: _____

UX PROJECT NAME: _____

COMPETITOR A: _____

COMPETITOR B: _____

FACTOR	MY BUSINESS	STRENGTH	WEAKNESS	COMPETITOR A	COMPETITOR B
Products					
Price					
Quality					
Selection					
Service					
Reliability					
Stability					
Expertise					
Company Reputation					
Location					
Appearance					
Sales Method					
Credit Policies					
Advertising					
Image					

COMPETITIVE ANALYSIS

DATE: _____

COMPETITOR A: _____

UX PROJECT NAME: _____

COMPETITOR B: _____

FACTOR	MY BUSINESS	STRENGTH	WEAKNESS	COMPETITOR A	COMPETITOR B
Products					
Price					
Quality					
Selection					
Service					
Reliability					
Stability					
Expertise					
Company Reputation					
Location					
Appearance					
Sales Method					
Credit Policies					
Advertising					
Image					

COMPETITIVE ANALYSIS

DATE: _____

COMPETITOR A: _____

UX PROJECT NAME: _____

COMPETITOR B: _____

FACTOR	MY BUSINESS	STRENGTH	WEAKNESS	COMPETITOR A	COMPETITOR B
Products					
Price					
Quality					
Selection					
Service					
Reliability					
Stability					
Expertise					
Company Reputation					
Location					
Appearance					
Sales Method					
Credit Policies					
Advertising					
Image					

COMPETITIVE ANALYSIS

DATE: _____

COMPETITOR A: _____

UX PROJECT NAME: _____

COMPETITOR B: _____

FACTOR	MY BUSINESS	STRENGTH	WEAKNESS	COMPETITOR A	COMPETITOR B
Products					
Price					
Quality					
Selection					
Service					
Reliability					
Stability					
Expertise					
Company Reputation					
Location					
Appearance					
Sales Method					
Credit Policies					
Advertising					
Image					

COMPETITIVE ANALYSIS

DATE: _____

COMPETITOR A: _____

UX PROJECT NAME: _____

COMPETITOR B: _____

FACTOR	MY BUSINESS	STRENGTH	WEAKNESS	COMPETITOR A	COMPETITOR B
Products					
Price					
Quality					
Selection					
Service					
Reliability					
Stability					
Expertise					
Company Reputation					
Location					
Appearance					
Sales Method					
Credit Policies					
Advertising					
Image					

COMPETITIVE ANALYSIS

DATE: _____

COMPETITOR A: _____

UX PROJECT NAME: _____

COMPETITOR B: _____

FACTOR	MY BUSINESS	STRENGTH	WEAKNESS	COMPETITOR A	COMPETITOR B
Products					
Price					
Quality					
Selection					
Service					
Reliability					
Stability					
Expertise					
Company Reputation					
Location					
Appearance					
Sales Method					
Credit Policies					
Advertising					
Image					

COMPETITIVE ANALYSIS

DATE: _____

COMPETITOR A: _____

UX PROJECT NAME: _____

COMPETITOR B: _____

FACTOR	MY BUSINESS	STRENGTH	WEAKNESS	COMPETITOR A	COMPETITOR B
Products					
Price					
Quality					
Selection					
Service					
Reliability					
Stability					
Expertise					
Company Reputation					
Location					
Appearance					
Sales Method					
Credit Policies					
Advertising					
Image					

COMPETITIVE ANALYSIS

DATE: _____

UX PROJECT NAME: _____

COMPETITOR A: _____

COMPETITOR B: _____

FACTOR	MY BUSINESS	STRENGTH	WEAKNESS	COMPETITOR A	COMPETITOR B
Products					
Price					
Quality					
Selection					
Service					
Reliability					
Stability					
Expertise					
Company Reputation					
Location					
Appearance					
Sales Method					
Credit Policies					
Advertising					
Image					

COMPETITIVE ANALYSIS

DATE: _____

UX PROJECT NAME: _____

COMPETITOR A: _____

COMPETITOR B: _____

FACTOR	MY BUSINESS	STRENGTH	WEAKNESS	COMPETITOR A	COMPETITOR B
Products					
Price					
Quality					
Selection					
Service					
Reliability					
Stability					
Expertise					
Company Reputation					
Location					
Appearance					
Sales Method					
Credit Policies					
Advertising					
Image					

COMPETITIVE ANALYSIS

DATE: _____

COMPETITOR A: _____

UX PROJECT NAME: _____

COMPETITOR B: _____

FACTOR	MY BUSINESS	STRENGTH	WEAKNESS	COMPETITOR A	COMPETITOR B
Products					
Price					
Quality					
Selection					
Service					
Reliability					
Stability					
Expertise					
Company Reputation					
Location					
Appearance					
Sales Method					
Credit Policies					
Advertising					
Image					

COMPETITIVE ANALYSIS

DATE: _____

COMPETITOR A: _____

UX PROJECT NAME: _____

COMPETITOR B: _____

FACTOR	MY BUSINESS	STRENGTH	WEAKNESS	COMPETITOR A	COMPETITOR B
Products					
Price					
Quality					
Selection					
Service					
Reliability					
Stability					
Expertise					
Company Reputation					
Location					
Appearance					
Sales Method					
Credit Policies					
Advertising					
Image					

COMPETITIVE ANALYSIS

DATE: _____

COMPETITOR A: _____

UX PROJECT NAME: _____

COMPETITOR B: _____

FACTOR	MY BUSINESS	STRENGTH	WEAKNESS	COMPETITOR A	COMPETITOR B
Products					
Price					
Quality					
Selection					
Service					
Reliability					
Stability					
Expertise					
Company Reputation					
Location					
Appearance					
Sales Method					
Credit Policies					
Advertising					
Image					

COMPETITIVE ANALYSIS

DATE: _____

COMPETITOR A: _____

UX PROJECT NAME: _____

COMPETITOR B: _____

FACTOR	MY BUSINESS	STRENGTH	WEAKNESS	COMPETITOR A	COMPETITOR B
Products					
Price					
Quality					
Selection					
Service					
Reliability					
Stability					
Expertise					
Company Reputation					
Location					
Appearance					
Sales Method					
Credit Policies					
Advertising					
Image					

COMPETITIVE ANALYSIS

DATE: _____   COMPETITOR A: _____

UX PROJECT NAME: _____   COMPETITOR B: _____

FACTOR	MY BUSINESS	STRENGTH	WEAKNESS	COMPETITOR A	COMPETITOR B
Products					
Price					
Quality					
Selection					
Service					
Reliability					
Stability					
Expertise					
Company Reputation					
Location					
Appearance					
Sales Method					
Credit Policies					
Advertising					
Image					

COMPETITIVE ANALYSIS

DATE: _____

COMPETITOR A: _____

UX PROJECT NAME: _____

COMPETITOR B: _____

FACTOR	MY BUSINESS	STRENGTH	WEAKNESS	COMPETITOR A	COMPETITOR B
Products					
Price					
Quality					
Selection					
Service					
Reliability					
Stability					
Expertise					
Company Reputation					
Location					
Appearance					
Sales Method					
Credit Policies					
Advertising					
Image					

COMPETITIVE ANALYSIS

DATE : _____

UX PROJECT NAME: _____

COMPETITOR A : _____

COMPETITOR B : _____

FACTOR	MY BUSINESS	STRENGTH	WEAKNESS	COMPETITOR A	COMPETITOR B
Products					
Price					
Quality					
Selection					
Service					
Reliability					
Stability					
Expertise					
Company Reputation					
Location					
Appearance					
Sales Method					
Credit Policies					
Advertising					
Image					

COMPETITIVE ANALYSIS

DATE: _____

COMPETITOR A: _____

UX PROJECT NAME: _____

COMPETITOR B: _____

FACTOR	MY BUSINESS	STRENGTH	WEAKNESS	COMPETITOR A	COMPETITOR B
Products					
Price					
Quality					
Selection					
Service					
Reliability					
Stability					
Expertise					
Company Reputation					
Location					
Appearance					
Sales Method					
Credit Policies					
Advertising					
Image					

COMPETITIVE ANALYSIS

DATE: _____   COMPETITOR A: _____

UX PROJECT NAME: _____   COMPETITOR B: _____

FACTOR	MY BUSINESS	STRENGTH	WEAKNESS	COMPETITOR A	COMPETITOR B
Products					
Price					
Quality					
Selection					
Service					
Reliability					
Stability					
Expertise					
Company Reputation					
Location					
Appearance					
Sales Method					
Credit Policies					
Advertising					
Image					

COMPETITIVE ANALYSIS

DATE : _____   COMPETITOR A : _____

UX PROJECT NAME : _____   COMPETITOR B : _____

FACTOR	MY BUSINESS	STRENGTH	WEAKNESS	COMPETITOR A	COMPETITOR B
Products					
Price					
Quality					
Selection					
Service					
Reliability					
Stability					
Expertise					
Company Reputation					
Location					
Appearance					
Sales Method					
Credit Policies					
Advertising					
Image					

COMPETITIVE ANALYSIS

DATE: _____

COMPETITOR A: _____

UX PROJECT NAME: _____

COMPETITOR B: _____

FACTOR	MY BUSINESS	STRENGTH	WEAKNESS	COMPETITOR A	COMPETITOR B
Products					
Price					
Quality					
Selection					
Service					
Reliability					
Stability					
Expertise					
Company Reputation					
Location					
Appearance					
Sales Method					
Credit Policies					
Advertising					
Image					

COMPETITIVE ANALYSIS

DATE : _____

COMPETITOR A : _____

UX PROJECT NAME: _____

COMPETITOR B : _____

FACTOR	MY BUSINESS	STRENGTH	WEAKNESS	COMPETITOR A	COMPETITOR B
Products					
Price					
Quality					
Selection					
Service					
Reliability					
Stability					
Expertise					
Company Reputation					
Location					
Appearance					
Sales Method					
Credit Policies					
Advertising					
Image					

COMPETITIVE ANALYSIS

DATE: _____

UX PROJECT NAME: _____

COMPETITOR A: _____

COMPETITOR B: _____

FACTOR	MY BUSINESS	STRENGTH	WEAKNESS	COMPETITOR A	COMPETITOR B
Products					
Price					
Quality					
Selection					
Service					
Reliability					
Stability					
Expertise					
Company Reputation					
Location					
Appearance					
Sales Method					
Credit Policies					
Advertising					
Image					

COMPETITIVE ANALYSIS

DATE: _____

COMPETITOR A: _____

UX PROJECT NAME: _____

COMPETITOR B: _____

FACTOR	MY BUSINESS	STRENGTH	WEAKNESS	COMPETITOR A	COMPETITOR B
Products					
Price					
Quality					
Selection					
Service					
Reliability					
Stability					
Expertise					
Company Reputation					
Location					
Appearance					
Sales Method					
Credit Policies					
Advertising					
Image					

COMPETITIVE ANALYSIS

DATE: _____

COMPETITOR A: _____

UX PROJECT NAME: _____

COMPETITOR B: _____

FACTOR	MY BUSINESS	STRENGTH	WEAKNESS	COMPETITOR A	COMPETITOR B
Products					
Price					
Quality					
Selection					
Service					
Reliability					
Stability					
Expertise					
Company Reputation					
Location					
Appearance					
Sales Method					
Credit Policies					
Advertising					
Image					

COMPETITIVE ANALYSIS

DATE: _____   COMPETITOR A: _____

UX PROJECT NAME: _____   COMPETITOR B: _____

FACTOR	MY BUSINESS	STRENGTH	WEAKNESS	COMPETITOR A	COMPETITOR B
Products					
Price					
Quality					
Selection					
Service					
Reliability					
Stability					
Expertise					
Company Reputation					
Location					
Appearance					
Sales Method					
Credit Policies					
Advertising					
Image					

COMPETITIVE ANALYSIS

DATE: _____

COMPETITOR A: _____

UX PROJECT NAME: _____

COMPETITOR B: _____

FACTOR	MY BUSINESS	STRENGTH	WEAKNESS	COMPETITOR A	COMPETITOR B
Products					
Price					
Quality					
Selection					
Service					
Reliability					
Stability					
Expertise					
Company Reputation					
Location					
Appearance					
Sales Method					
Credit Policies					
Advertising					
Image					

COMPETITIVE ANALYSIS

DATE: _____   COMPETITOR A: _____

UX PROJECT NAME: _____   COMPETITOR B: _____

FACTOR	MY BUSINESS	STRENGTH	WEAKNESS	COMPETITOR A	COMPETITOR B
Products					
Price					
Quality					
Selection					
Service					
Reliability					
Stability					
Expertise					
Company Reputation					
Location					
Appearance					
Sales Method					
Credit Policies					
Advertising					
Image					

COMPETITIVE ANALYSIS

DATE: _____

COMPETITOR A: _____

UX PROJECT NAME: _____

COMPETITOR B: _____

FACTOR	MY BUSINESS	STRENGTH	WEAKNESS	COMPETITOR A	COMPETITOR B
Products					
Price					
Quality					
Selection					
Service					
Reliability					
Stability					
Expertise					
Company Reputation					
Location					
Appearance					
Sales Method					
Credit Policies					
Advertising					
Image					

Takeaway notes:

_____

_____

_____

_____

_____

Year of use:

_____